Great Things Happen
WHEN GIRLS DREAM

A Collaboration Led By

Regina Sunshine Robinson

Book 2 of the Awesome Girl Book Series

Copyright © 2020 Regina "Sunshine" Robinson

All rights reserved.

Published by the Regina Sunshine Global Network, LLC

Cover Design by Darshawne Wickerson
Character Design by Olivia Elizabeth Stanley
Editing by Kathryn Stanley
Editing by Pamelia Gore Stanley
Logo Design by Kristen Culbreath

All Rights Reserved. No part or portion of this publication may be reproduced, stored in a retrieval system, or transmitted in any form or by any means - electronic, mechanical, photocopying, recording, or otherwise - without the express written consent of the author.

For information:
Regina Sunshine Global Network, LLC
www.ReginaSunshine.com

ISBN: 978-1-7359384-0-0 Paperback
ISBN: 978-1-7359384-1-7 Ebook

When Girls Dream

DEDICATION

I'm from a little town in North Carolina called Tabor City. So much of the world seemed big and out of reach to a little black girl like me. One of the biggest things that changed my life was attending North Carolina A & T State University. It was there where I saw people that looked just like me from all walks of life achieving at the highest level. My mom and my grandmother specifically had always told me that I could do great things in this world. It was at A&T where I could truly touch the dream.

I had planned to attend North Carolina State on a Chemical Engineering scholarship. But one trip to A&T, and I was in love. That trip watered a seed that had been planted in me by two phenomenal women: Ms. Elizabeth Taylor and Dr. Maudie Davis.

Ms. Taylor and Dr. Davis were two black female educators at my high school who were also A&T alumni. They were two of the toughest teachers in the school, especially on me. But they loved me too. And they planted the A&T seed in my heart. They inspired me, pushed me, encouraged me, and they were forever talking about their love of their precious Aggie Land and that Blue & Gold. In fact, it was from Ms. Taylor that I first heard the words, "Aggie born. Aggie bred. When I die, I'll be Aggie dead." These two women were true forces of change, and not only did they work hard to make sure I was living up to my full potential, they were always watering what they had planted about A&T in my life.

So, thank you, Ms. Elizabeth Taylor and Dr. Maudie Davis, for being the instruments of so much good in my life. Thank you for challenging me to be better, especially when I didn't understand it. Thank you for never accepting average. Thank you for setting a standard that seemed unattainable but kept me striving. Thank you for being true examples of black female excellence and Black Girl Magic before that term was even coined. Because of the seeds you planted in my life, I am living my dreams and taking a whole generation of other girls with me.

I dedicate this book to you in the same way you dedicated your lives to all of us who sat in your classrooms and roamed through your halls. You were unwavering in your efforts and your sacrifices have borne much fruit.

AGGIE PRIDE!

Regina Sunshine Robinson

When Girls Dream

TABLE OF CONTENTS

ACKNOWLEDGEMENTS

INTRODUCTION 1

JANAE KANU - WHEN GIRLS DREAM POEM 4

1. SOMMER DAINA BUTLER 6
2. KANURI ELISE FOWLER -YIKEALO 8
3. LEILA A'DELL SHI'ANNA GRAYDEN 12
4. OLIVIA ELIZABETH STANLEY 16
5. DE'ZYRE WILLIAMS 18
6. AALIYAH SKYE ROBERTSON 22
7. MILAN RICHELLE WALLER 26
8. ZAYDAH LOTALLAH 30
9. GABRIELLA NIQUASHIA SKELTON 34
10. JOY MCKENZIE WRIGHT 36
11. MARLEY RANDOLPH 38
12. ALEJANDRA STACK 40
13. MAKAYLA COLEMAN 44
14. ZOE PATSY GORE 48

ANTONIA WILLIAMS – AWESOME GIRL POEM 50

"IT'S NOT OVER TIL YOU WIN!"

Regina Sunshine Robinson

INTRODUCTION

When we launched the first Awesome Girl book in 2019, we knew immediately there would be more books. From the joy on the faces of the girls to the words of encouragement from their parents, it was obvious that we needed to allow other girls this opportunity to share their hearts and their dreams. It is my dream that one day we'll have girls from every corner of the world as authors in our Awesome Girl books. I want to know what they dream about and how their dreams will impact the world. It is our dreams that keep pushing us forward and light up our days. All it takes is one dream to change the world, and just maybe, one of our girls is the dreamer the world is waiting for because we all know that great things happen "When Girls Dream!"

Remember this….

- ✓ God loves you just the way you are.
- ✓ You are beautiful because you were created in love.
- ✓ You are fearfully and wonderfully made.
- ✓ You have the seeds of greatness within you.
- ✓ You were born to live a victorious life.
- ✓ You are brilliant, gorgeous, talented, and fabulous.
- ✓ You are worthy of the best things in life.
- ✓ And one more thing……It's Not Over Til You Win!

When Girls Dream
A poem by Janae Kanu

I am a black girl who dreams
Why is that so important
Because through my dreams, I can change the world
And so can you

When girls dream, they soar incredible heights
When girls dream, they can end racial fights
Girls can make a huge impact because of dreams
Even though your dreams aren't what they seem
You can be a doctor, teacher, writer, actor, singer, dancer, chef
You can even be the president
You can dream big or you can dream small
All you have to do is see it through

Just have to close your eyes and believe it's true
Believe in what you can do even when it seems impossible to you

We are girls who dream
Why is that so important
Because through our dreams, we can change the world
And it doesn't start with just one girl

It starts with me
It starts with you
And in your heart, you know it's true
That we can do anything we put our minds to

When you dream, strive for the best
And don't ever settle for less
So hold your head up high
Because when you believe, our dreams can reach the sky

Bio

Janae Kanu is a 12-year-old actress, model, spoken word artist, student, dreamer, and change advocate. As the oldest of five, she is a natural born leader and problem solver. Starting from the age of 5, she was in school plays, and soon after when she moved to Georgia, she started modeling at the age of 9. She has also been a finalist in a nationwide competition and is the female lead in her current school film. Janae enjoys cooking, singing, getting good grades, and spending time with her family and friends.

CHAPTER 1

SOMMER DAINA BUTLER

Age: 6

When Girls Dream

I dream of changing the world. If I could, I would stop people from dying. Everybody is getting sick and trying to stay alive. People die every day and one day I want to stop that. I would make sure people would stay at home. We would have pajama day every day.

I dream of having everything in the garden that I grow. Except, I don't like hot peppers. I really like strawberries. I love peaches and apples. I also love grapes. I love broccoli and cheese as well.

I look up to my mommy. She teaches me stuff, lots of stuff. Girls rule the world and girls are the best. I look up to my daddy. We play chess and make slushies. We own a moonwalk service. I want to own a daycare one day so I can help teach younger girls how to win.

If I could give advice to younger girls, I would tell them to always be positive and do your homework even though I don't like homework.

When I get older, I'm going to buy a mansion with 20 rooms. It's going to have a pool and a hot tub. I'm going to go to the Olympics because I am the best swimmer. That's how I'm going to pay for these things.

Bio

Sommer Butler is a 6-year-old currently being home schooled. When she grows up, she wants to be a dentist. She also wants to be an Olympic swimmer and gymnast. Sommer is the daughter of author and activist, Dainhen Butler and business owner, Crystal Brown.

CHAPTER 2

KANURI ELISE FOWLER-YIKEALO

Age: 8

When Girls Dream

I am an eight-year-old girl and I usually dream about rainbows, *My Little Pony*, and unicorns. These are my favorite things I have all around me when I am not dreaming. I try to make my life as happy as my dreams, but through my eyes, life is not always whimsical as it might seem to be in a fairytale world. I will discuss three different dreams that are important to me.

My most important memory in

my dream is my mom. She makes me feel happy. She cares about me and makes sure I am safe. Her hugs make me feel excited and I laugh out loud. She reminds me of Bailey in the movie, *A Dog's Journey*. Bailey, the dog in the movie, was always there to protect the little girl C.J.

Second, I can remember a dream where giant spiders were chasing me. I tried all I could to get away from them. I kept running and running and running until I saw this hole to hide. There was a lot of dirt around the hole, so I began to build blocks as high as the sky. The spiders could not climb on the blocks because their legs were too short. I had gotten away and built a sky home, and this was my space to feel safe until I heard my mom saying, "Nuri, wake up." She said I was talking in my sleep (smile).

Third, I had a dream about the virus in our world. I was listening to the news when I heard about many people being sick and dying from the virus. In my dream, I began to feel sad. I saw very sick people in the hospital, and it made me think about my family, friends, and people all over the world. In this dream, I found myself encouraging people to help others. Also, I told people how important it was to wear masks, wash hands and be safe. So, when I woke out of the dream with tears, I felt sorry for the people who were getting sick and I could not help them.

Lastly, dreams are so important to our daily lives. Sometimes dreams are hopeful, sometimes dreams are scary, and sometimes dreams bring a lot of comfort. I am happy that God has blessed me to keep on dreaming. I do believe that my dreams will come true and God will continue to keep me safe, provide me protection, and allow me to help others.

Bio

Kanuri Elise Fowler-Yikealo is an eight-year-old scholar at Victory World Church Christian School. She is the daughter of Dr. Jillian Whatley and Oluyemi Fowler-Yikealo. Kanuri is a Girl Scout who also participates in Diamonds in the Rough, Victory World Church Step Team, Victory World Church Christian School Art Club and performs ballet and tap with Dance Phusion. She dreams of helping homeless people, providing food for them so they won't be hungry. Kanuri is also interested in social justice and helping communities to treat all races fairly. She would also like to invent a game, Wonderland, using coding. These activities have helped Kanuri develop lasting friendships and introduced her to great adult mentors such as her teacher, Wilma, who passed away in 2019 and from whom Kanuri learned many life lessons. Wilma was Kanuri's hero on earth; now she is her hero in heaven.

"You don't have to stay in the dark and hide in the shadows of life. Get out there and be free girl do what you want and be what you want to be."- Kanuri Elise Fowler-Yikealo

CHAPTER 3

LEILA A'DELL SHI'ANNA GRAYDEN

Age: 9

When Girls Dream

My name is Leila Grayden. I am 9 years old and I am going to the fourth grade. I like to play outside and ride my bike. My favorite things to do is play with dogs, comb my doll's hair, ride my bike, and read books. My favorite food is macaroni and cheese and blueberries. I am a girl with big dreams. I dream a lot at night. Sometimes I have funny, happy, and even scary dreams at night. When I am not sleeping, I still have dreams. I dream of things I like to do. I enjoy praying for people and spreading love. I like to make people laugh. My dream is to help those in need. There are many people in the world that need food, clothes, and even a house to live in. Some people sometimes do not get food, or water, and things they need each day. Many people in the world are hurting. Sometimes you see people crying and it is because they are hurt. We had a tornado to come to where we live. The tornado knocked down a lot of trees and fell on people's houses. Some people could not live in their houses after that. We went and helped some people and gave them food and water. My dream is to keep helping people. When I grow up, I want to help everybody. We all need a house, food, beds, and children need toys and books.

I believe my dreams can change the world. I dream of having my own school. In my school there will be boys and girl everywhere. They will learn how to spell, read, write in cursive, and how to play instruments. Everybody will be learning to read and do math. If the words get too hard, we will help them learn how to say them and spell them. There will not be mean people at my school. We will show love for each other and be very nice. All the teachers will be nice and give the kids big hugs. We will have good healthy food for them to eat every day. My Namma said some little children do not get to eat sometimes. We will have good food at my school so everybody can be healthy and strong. In my dream my school is very big. If you have a big school a lot of kids can come. I want everybody to come to my school so I can help them. If we help a lot of children, they will help a lot of other children. If people see you do good things, then they will want to do good things too. If the whole world does good things, then we will all be better people.

I dream also of being a veterinarian. I love dogs. My dad has a lot of dogs. Their names are Pabalo and Gucc. I like playing with them. My Auntie Jayla has a dog too. His name is Ziggie. Ziggie is always running all over the place. I like playing with the dogs and rubbing their hair. When I become a veterinarian, I will have to give the dogs a shot, so they will not get sick. If they get hurt, I will have to give them some medicine too. I dream of combing the dog's hair and putting hair bows on the girl dogs. They can have pink and white hairbows like the Jo-Jo Siwa bows. I can paint their fingernails. Dogs can be good friends to people.

It is okay to dream. It does not matter whether you have a big dream or not so big dream. When we dream of things that we like to do we should write them down, so we do not forget them or tell someone. I want to accomplish all my dreams. I will never give up and I will always do my best.

Leila's Affirmations
1. Always believe in yourself and never give up.
2. Always do your best.

Bio
Leila A'Dell Shi'Anna Grayden lives in Seneca, SC. She lives with her Papa, Namma, and her little sister Leena. Leila is going to the fourth grade. She wants to preach the gospel, write books, and learn to play the guitar. Leila loves dogs and wants to be "a dog doctor". She enjoys going to her dad's and playing with the dogs. Leila loves her sisters and loves playing with her friends. Leila enjoys people and likes to laugh. She has a super big heart and always gives the best hugs. Leila wants to go to college and become a teacher. Leila is a Phenomenal Girl!!

When Girls Dream

CHAPTER 4

OLIVIA ELIZABETH STANLEY

Age: 9

When Girls Dream

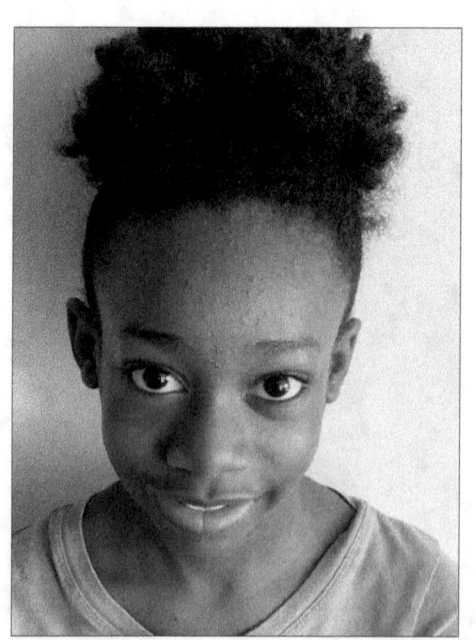

I dream of changing the world through using my gifts and talents to not just serve but also provide for those people in need. One of the things I would like to do is sew masks to give to people during this pandemic to help keep them safe. I also dream of growing fresh fruits and vegetables in a community garden. The purpose of the community garden is to provide healthy food to homeless people and to children and families who live in poverty. I dream of one day being a clothing designer. Sewing clothes is my passion. As a clothing designer I can also make clothes and give them to people who don't have them or cannot afford to buy them.

I think girls can change the world simply by being their true selves. By being your true self, you show others what confidence looks like. You also show others that it is ok for them to be themselves. It teaches people to embrace and love who and how God created them to be. Dreams are important for girls. Dreams are what is in your heart. When you pursue your dreams, others can see your dreams and purpose. They learn it is ok for them to follow their dreams.

I admire Regina Sunshine Robinson. She is brave and confident. She has written books to inspire girls and women to follow their dreams. She shows love by helping other people pursue their dreams. When she speaks to groups of girls, she tells them they are smart, brilliant, and worthy. She also tells them that they will grow up to be strong women who change the world. She reminds me that it is ok to dream. I now believe anything is possible. I am going to be LEGENDARY!

Affirmations
I am beautiful just the way I am.
Never be Afraid because God is With You!
I trust God!
I have Faith in God!
I Expect God!

Bio
Olivia Elizabeth Stanley was born in Cary, NC on March 25, 2011. She is the daughter of Oliver and Pamelia Stanley. Olivia loves to sing, sew, draw, and read. She attends Grace Christian School in Raleigh, NC. She is a published author and illustrator. She is also an owner and designer at OES Designs where she makes doll clothing and accessories. Her goal when she grows up is to be legendary!

CHAPTER 5

DE'ZYRE WILLIAMS

Age: 9

When Girls Dream

A dream may be composed of a lot of thoughts that one may have. Dreaming is a common thing to do. When you have a dream, it means that there is something positive that you have a desire to come true. It is always possible that dreams will come true. This is only factual if you put in the work to make it happen. I have always dreamed of being an author and owning my own business. I worked until I made that dream come true. This is an example of what you can do to make your dreams come true.

To go further, when girls dream, they may dream about so many different things. Some of the dreams may include but are not limited to what you desire to be when you grow up, what college that you want to attend, wanting to become famous, and so forth. Working hard is the key to carrying out your dreams.

There is a special woman that taught me that working hard and believing in my dreams was possible. My mommy is the special woman that I admire because she is my superhero and has always shown me that hard work will always pay off if I believe and have faith. She has always worked hard to make sure that I achieved my dreams. Her dreams of making a change in society has always inspired me to do the same. This is how I became a literacy advocate. Learning and enjoying reading is a dream that I have for all children because it can change the world. I saw that the world continues to struggle with being literate, so I decided to become an author. As an author, I use my platform to encourage other children to enjoy reading.

As you can see, when a girl dreams, she is powerful and fearless. Girls will strive until they accomplish their dreams. When a girl dreams, it puts her into a happy place that allows her mind and imagination to run wild. You will never know where the mind and dreams of a girl will take her. Girls, please believe that dreams can change and save lives and that your dreams are powerful.

Lastly, A good rule of thumb is to write down your dreams so that you know what your dreams are and mark them off as you complete them. Girls have so many things ahead of them in life that they can achieve. Some of the things that girls have ahead of them is that they have opportunities to get a good education, have a great job, and enjoy being a girl. My advice to all girls is to always believe in your dreams and never let anyone tell you what you cannot do! Girls Rock! Whenever you are having a reservation to carry out your dream, always remember this quote by Walt Disney, "If you can dream it, you can do it."

Bio

De'Zyre (pronounced Desire) Williams is a 9-year-old author, youth inspirational speaker, entrepreneur, and a 2019 Awesome Girl. She is a native of North Carolina and a rising fourth grader that is taking accelerated Academically and Intellectually Gift (AIG) coursework. De'Zyre's hobbies are writing, reading, martial arts and gymnastics trainings, playing ROBLOX and spending time with her mother and the rest of her family. You may find out more about De'Zyre by visiting her website at www.dezyrewilliams.com.

When Girls Dream

CHAPTER 6

AALIYAH SKYE ROBERTSON

Age: 10

When Girls Dream

When girls dream, lives can be healed, new technology can be created, the planet can be cleaned, and animals can be saved. You see, I know this because there are girls that dreamed and became very important people on this earth. Girls that are doctors, engineers, scientist, politicians, vets, and much more. My dream is to become a vet, so I can help and care for hurt and sick animals of all kinds. I also dream to be a paleontologist so I can learn about life in the past by finding fossils. Some women that I admire that followed their dreams are Serena and Venus Williams. They were the first black women to win first place in tennis. Venus and Serena Williams inspired other black women to play tennis too and also go for their dreams. Girls who dream break barriers and make a way for others, and my dream is to do the same. I want to be the best I can be in whatever I become. I want to make sure that other black girls behind me know that their dreams and lives matter and to never give up on what is important to their hearts.

I have three younger sisters who are important to me. I love them so much and they look up to me and follow me around all of the time. I want to inspire them to dream and to know that with God by their side, anything is possible. I watch my 7-year-old sister dance all the time at church and she loves to dance. I want her dreams to come true and watch her become the best that she can be. Together we can be successful in the world and make a difference just by being us. I always enjoy being different. I am not like other girls who like girly things. I like dinosaurs, writing, reading, and playing video games and I think I am pretty awesome. No matter what you are into never change who you are because others don't understand you. The world is beautiful because we are all unique. So, keep dreaming!

Affirmation Statements
1. Never give up on your dreams.
2. You are beautiful the way you are.
3. You are loved.
4. You are worthy.
5. Let what makes you unique shine.

Bio
Aaliyah Skye Robertson is a 10-year-old scholar who loves animals, video games, dinosaurs, reading and writing. Aaliyah is shy with a big heart and big dreams. Aaliyah is the oldest of four girls and is a natural

leader who doesn't tolerate nonsense. Aaliyah loves the outdoors, family movie nights, and spending time with the people she loves.

When Girls Dream

CHAPTER 7

MILAN RICHELLE WALLER

Age: 10

When Girls Dream

I dream of changing the world in my pursuit of a career in engineering and medicine. With my first love -- cooking and my second love -- math and science, I am focused on developing biomedical technology that will assist people and pets with affordable prosthetics to live a long, prosperous, and functional quality of life. Harriet Tubman once said, "Every great dream begins with a dreamer. Always remember, you have within you, the strength, the patience, and the passion for reaching for the stars to change the world." I am that dreamer!

I dream of becoming a biomedical engineer that practices medicine. I desire to change people's perspectives and world views about people and pets with disabilities as well as the potential of young African American woman. As a girl impacted by an invisible disability, I need to be the change that I want to see in the world by creating assistive technology to help others on their journey to live life more abundantly despite being differently-abled.

I look at the world and the transformation of girls' dreams and how they have changed the world by simply following their hearts and passions as advocates for change. For example, I LOVE the story of Malala Yousafzai. Malala made international headlines in 2012 when, at just 15 years old, she was shot in the head by the Taliban for advocating girls' education. Surviving the attack, she continues her efforts to ensure girls worldwide have access to quality education and equal rights.

I admire Justice Ruth Bader Ginsburg, a woman who made an impact by advocating for women's rights. I loved it when she said, "When I'm sometimes asked when will there be enough women on the Supreme Court and I say, 'When there are nine,' people are shocked. But there'd been nine men, and nobody's ever raised a question about that. That's why fighting for women's rights is essential."

I also admire Dr. Treena Livingston Arinzeh, a black physicist, biomedical engineer and, professor known for her work researching adult stem-cell therapy. Dr. Arinzeh developed the first Tissue Engineering and Applied Biomaterials Laboratory at NJIT in the fall of 2001. Because of her dreams, I can dream big and soar in the field of biomedical engineering.

I believe girls can change the world together because every girl is different. With all of our dreams and goals together, we can change the world forever for those that come behind us, which is what it's all about.

Dreams are essential for girls because dreams are inspired thoughts. If we can see the dream in our minds, we possess the power to control the dream and bring it to fruition with our hard work, emotions, and images (vision boards).

I know dreams can change and save lives, because when I become Dr. Milan R. Waller, biomedical engineer, and veterinarian, I will save lives physically and qualitatively with assistive technology. I will continue to chase this dream until this dream chases me.

Affirmations
- I am the head and not the tail.
- I am love, created in God's image.
- I give love and grace to myself and others with nothing expected in return.
- I am fearfully and wonderfully made, marvelous in HIS eyes.
- I am a walking miracle and a magnet for blessings and prosperity.
- I am Dr. Milan Waller!

Bio
Milan Waller, an entrepreneur, innovator, civic leader, and young trailblazer, hails from Atlanta, Georgia. She is the beloved daughter of Ms. Melissa Waller and a budding and bright seventh grader at The Wilson Academy in Conyers, Georgia. Milan seeks to raise awareness about medical issues impacting students with invisible disabilities, such as allergies, asthma, and eczema, all of which she has experienced firsthand. Milan has been recognized by the Madam CJ Walker Legacy Foundation, Girl Scouts of USA, Victory World Christian School, and Junior League of Atlanta for her entrepreneurial spirit, tenacity, business acumen, volunteer work, civic leadership, and uncompromising devotion to her faith.

CHAPTER 8

ZAYDAH LOTALLAH

Age: 11

When Girls Dream

When girls dream, they create new possibilities.

Madam C.J. Walker, an African American woman, dreamed. Even when the whole world said she couldn't do something, she kept on dreaming. When she wanted to give up, she never did because she knew the power of a dream was the only thing she needed. All of the dreams, the blood, sweat, and tears helped her become

America's first self-made female millionaire. She used a struggle, hair loss in her case, and turned it in to a positive motivator. She taught women that they were beautiful and that they could also rule the world. She dreamed and helped to spread kindness. You can, too.

We all have a dream, whether it's to invent the next big thing or if it's to help sick animals. Wonderful things can happen when you dream. Spreading happiness to the world is what a dream could do. Loving on our brothers and sisters and uplifting them so that they, too, can dream.

But dreams are just the beginning. The action you choose to take is your choice, but you have to make sure you take that action. Make your dreams real. Be the best person you can be. Be the YOU that accomplishes your dreams. Everyone has it in them. Some people need extra help seeing their worth. Once you find yours you can help someone else find his or hers.

I am a dreamer too, and yes, it is tough when things don't work out. But one thing we can never do is give up. I have an acting career that is moving slower than expected, but I haven't given up on it. If I do, I will never know what will happen. I keep trying so that one day I DO find out what is going to happen.

You should keep trying too, because the thing about dreams is you never know when they are just about to come true. That's why we can't ever give up. The world needs you.

Affirmations
1. I attract good people into my life.
2. I have people who love me even in hard times.
3. I am getting closer to my dreams every day.
4. I am beautiful and unique just the way I am.
5. I love myself and do the best I can every day.

Bio

Zaydah Lotallah is a speaker, actress, singer, and author all while maintaining excellent grades in elementary school (heading into middle). Zaydah hopes to use these public skills and platforms to make the world a better place, especially in the areas of social justice and civil rights. Her greatest dream is to be President of the United States, so that she may have the greatest impact. While not at the White House yet, she lives just outside of Atlanta, GA with her parents and two younger brothers.

Connect with Zaydah via her website, www.zaydah.com, see what she's up to on YouTube @Zaydah Love or check out her Etsy slime shop, also called ZaydahLove.

When Girls Dream

CHAPTER 9

GABRIELLA NIQUASHIA SKELTON

Age: 12

When Girls Dream

When girls dream a lot of things can happen. I dream that serving will make a difference in the world. A lot of things need to be done to make the world better. I believe if everybody does a part it can be done. I am going to do my part. I´m going to help people. I am going to do my best in school and be a better person. I help them and then they will help somebody else. This will go on and my dream of the world being a better place will happen.

My dream of helping people is already coming true. I am part of an outreach program named Predestined Outreach. The program was started to help young people. It teaches us what service is. I see how other people may not live better than I do. It shows me ways of how to help them. We go out and serve the county, feed the homeless, help people fix homes by painting them, visit nursing homes, and play bingo with the elderly. We have cleaned an empty jailhouse that's going to be restored as a shelter. There was a tornado in Seneca, SC and then I helped hold signs up at Shaver Complex for the tornado victims and helped at Blue Ridge Community Field giving out water, food, clothes and other items. I dream of continuing to help people throughout my life.

I also dream of becoming a chef, FBI agent, own my own business, cheerleader, a dancer and be in the Army.

I AM Affirmations
- I am smart.
- I am pretty.
- I am helpful.
- I am loving.
- I am successful in school.

Bio

Gabriella Niquashia Skelton, called Gabby by friends and family, was born July 28, 2008. She lives in Seneca SC with her parents, Dennis and Theresa Skelton. She loves to sing and has been in the school chorus for three years, beginning at Blue Ridge Elementary School and now at Seneca Middle School where she sings alto.

Gabby loves serving God and people. She attends Richland Baptist church where she does praise dance and participates in Youth Sunday every fourth Sunday. She does announcements, presides, prays, reads scripture and ushers. She is also a part of an outreach program called, Predestined Outreach whose mission is to help young people. Gabby is also a member of the NAACP.

CHAPTER 10

JOY MCKENZIE WRIGHT

Age: 12

When Girls Dream

I'm a dream girl. I have so many hopes and dreams. I hope for a world where there is no human trafficking or poverty. And when I dream, here is what I see. I envision a world full of cures for sicknesses and disease. Sometimes all I do is daydream. I look into the sky and I take a journey to places that I create in my mind; places that are fun, colorful, and safe. I know that some dreams are not exactly real, but day dreaming is a way for me to think freely at times. Day dreaming is something that my mother has taught me to embrace, at least while I'm not doing schoolwork or other not so fun stuff around the house. And though my daydreams are about fantasy, my real dream is to change the world. I believe that girls can use their dreams to influence each other to do great things. Like, I love to swim. There is nothing I would rather do than to swim all day. So, one of my greatest dreams is to become an Olympic gold medalist. I want to show the world that brown girls aren't afraid of the water nor are we afraid to get our hair wet.

Dreams are important for girls because they give them life and courage to do great things. Girls dreams have been stolen and misused by so many people. We are often forced to do roles like cook and clean, but we are more than what the world thinks we should be. When girls dream, amazing inventions are created, and inspiring books are written. When a girl dreams, the world can see a brown girl use her power to do good. Our dreams prove that we are smart as boys and strong and brave like men. Our dreams give us opportunities to be powerful and that is what we need to run the world. When girls share their dreams with each other, it proves that exceptional things can happen. When girls dream, it sets an example that we can be great role models for other girls to do awesome things. That is why it is important for me to be a good example for future generations.

Another dream of mine is to be a lawyer. I dream of working in Congress one day to defend youth living in the foster care system and all people of color. I know I am special because I am adopted. There are so many young girls who will not get adopted and will spend most of their life in foster care. I dream of helping those girls to become strong like me and my mom. The world is so much bigger than what we all see. It's full of amazing girls from places that I want to visit one day. I hope that I am able to inspire other girls to dream beyond the stars. I believe dreams are important for girls because that is what dreams are made of, girls like me. I will always be a dream girl.

<u>Affirmation</u>: "Be positive and believe that you will make it through."

<u>Bio</u>
Joy Wright is a young entrepreneur. She loves her Doberman, Amani, swimming, reading, and baking sweet desserts with her dad. She believes in her power as a brown girl, and that no one can take that from her. For more about Joy, visit <u>www.sharejoygivehugs.com</u>.

CHAPTER 11

MARLEY RANDOLPH

Age: 12

When Girls Dream

When I dream, I dream of becoming a lawyer to help the wrongly convicted and traveling, especially to Hawaii.

In order for me to achieve my dreams, I need to work hard in school and focus on all my work. When I was younger, I thought that I would go to college and become a lawyer, and everything would be easy. But I learned that one needs to work hard and make good grades in school. This is why I do all my schoolwork and study hard to make good grades.

The way girls' dreams have changed

the world is amazing. Mae Jemison dreamed of being an astronaut and an engineer, then she became the first black woman to travel to space, an engineer and physician. She was able to do all of that because she worked hard in school and believed in herself. Minty Ross (you probably know her as Harriet Tubman) dreamed of black people being freed from slavery and slavery ending. Over the course of making her dream come true, she freed over 300 hundred slaves and made over 19 trips on the Underground Railroad. January 1, 1863 is when the Emancipation Proclamation was signed setting most slaves free and making Harriet's dream come true.

When I think about how I would be able to help people, travel, help my family and friends, it makes me feel good inside. All dreams are important because dreams are what the world was built on.

Affirmations
1. You can do it.
2. You are smart.
3. You are kind.
4. You are amazing!
5. You are beautiful.
6. I believe that you can do it if you work and believe in yourself.
7. Do not let anyone bring you down or tell you that you cannot because you can. I know that you can.

Bio
Marley Randolph was named after reggae legend, Bob Marley. Born May 3, 2008, she enjoys travelling and hopes to go to Hawaii someday. Her favorite animals are dogs and owls. *The Boondocks* is her favorite TV show. She's learning how to paint and hopes to get better by trying different techniques. Her dreams are to keep good grades throughout school, attend an HBCU, and become a lawyer.

CHAPTER 12

ALEJANDRA STACK

Age: 15

When Girls Dream

My name is Alejandra Stack. I'm 15 years old and currently reside in Atlanta Georgia. I am the CEO and founder of KidNewsMaker.com. KNM is a multimedia outlet that highlights any person under the age of 18 that is doing great things. Whether it be at school, in your community, or around the world, I want to highlight kids who make a difference and help other kids find inspiration in their peers and in themselves. Starting KNM is already a dream come true. Although my business is now global and has been recognized with multiple awards, it was a rough start.

Initially, I got the idea by flipping through magazines and newspapers while being bored at my mother's journalism job and noticing there really wasn't any news about kids, and if there was any at all, the kids were either already well established or they had just gotten into huge trouble. I asked my mother about it, and she told me if I wanted to see it, I would have to do it myself. It was a way for her to brush me off so she could get back to work. But I took her literally and went off to show her I could do just that.

I gathered a couple of friends to help and when I got back to her with a list of kids who I wanted to be featured, she was kind of shocked. At first, a lot of my mom's friends and some family members reposted a lot of my stuff so that helped a lot. I gave her an idea for a magazine design and used some money I earned from doing film work and a commercial to print my first copies.

It was amazing being able to actually hold my magazine in my own hands and then get ready to ship them. I really love sticking to a print publication, because in this day and age, a repost only takes a couple of seconds. I think other kids are a lot more thrilled when they can hold an article of themselves, and I feel as if kids who buy the magazine get a completely different perspective then they would by just clicking away at the screen and possibly getting distracted.

About 3 years into my business, things began moving a lot slower. I started gaining more competitors, and my mother and I were going through a pretty rough patch. She lost her job, and for about a year, we were living with other people. All of the money that we made went to food and down payments for any new place we could move into. Even though the articles on my website got around 2.7k views in a matter of a day or two, it seemed as if fewer and fewer people were donating and buying magazines. Not gonna lie, a small part of the reason why I wanted my business was for money I could earn by myself, and I was pretty disappointed when there weren't a lot of sales. Not only was it because I didn't get any money, but also because I thought there wasn't as much of a need for my product anymore.

For a moment, we seriously considered just giving up KidNewsMaker because we were putting in so much work only to get so little in return. A lot of people reached out saying they didn't want it to end. I never realized how many people actually cared about my business. It motivated my mom to open a donation page for people to help keep KidNewsMaker up, and we raised the first thousand in almost a day!

To add to that, I also got opportunities after opportunities to get more film projects and even ended up being directed by Tyler Perry in *Ruthless*, being the photo double for Abra in a Stephen King film *Dr. Sleep*, the sequel to *The Shining*, being on *The Walking Dead*, *Fear Street* and more.

I also got to network and became friends with some of the most amazing youth influencers, change-makers, actors, entrepreneurs and even ended up doing a four-state tour that led me to being a Truth Playmakers Awards honoree and ExCel Youth Award finalist.

It also helped a lot to have a village behind me backing me up, and of course, having my mom to guide me through these times. I have so much appreciation for her because even though we were going through what we were going through, she still found the time to help me fulfill my dreams. I'm also very appreciative of everyone who helped keep KNM alive, and my supporters now.

Today, my physical magazine copies are in The Bahamas, USA, Canada, Jamaica, Ireland, England, Australia, Nigeria and more. I've been recognized by media clubs and more.

The lesson I learned along the way? Make sure you never give up on yourself, know that it's okay to struggle and ask for help. It's a struggle getting through the dry patches in your business, and it's even harder getting through the ones in your life. But if you just keep the dream alive by simply believing, it goes a long way.

Bio

Alejandra Stack resides in Atlanta, Georgia. She is 15 years old, and the CEO and founder of KidNewsMaker.com, a multimedia outlet that highlights any person under the age of 18 that is doing great things. KNM's tagline is "We're not waiting, we're creating." Her magazine is distributed worldwide. Alejandra is also an actress who has appeared in a number movies and television shows. She has Bahamian roots, just like her favorite rock singer, Lenny Kravitz.

CHAPTER 13

MAKAYLA COLEMAN

Age: 16

When Girls Dream

When I was about six or seven, I got my first look at what I thought success looked like. She was a black doctor that lived in one of those really nice neighborhoods that you beg your parents to take you to trick-or-treat. She was a friend of my mom, and she was very kind. Since then, I think I've been subconsciously working to get where she is. I maintain good grades and stay out of trouble, but as I've gotten older, I've learned that success extends far past money. Don't get me wrong, I fully intend for money to be the least of my worries in the future, but success is more than that.

Success is positively affecting lives and doing work that hardly feels like a job. Something else that I've seen is that success is often directly related to a dream or passion. I've found that nothing good ever really happens on accident. Having a dream is like oiling a pan before pouring the cake batter in it. It may not be physically seen, but it's what makes the end result that much greater.

As far as me and my big dream, I honestly don't have it all figured out. I have three different professions of choice, and they change like every other month. I have definitely been dreaming though. I've been dreaming of making decisions that aren't subdued by fear, I've been dreaming of taking risks that come with reward, and I've been dreaming of creating a "new normal" for myself and others.

To an extent, I think I've been making a good effort at my dreams. This past school year, I tutored a student for the first time. I used to not be much of a talker, so this was new to me. It was with a young girl who was struggling in math. She started with a low grade and untapped potential, but she finished with a 94 and newfound confidence. It was already inside her, but it was rewarding to help bring it out. I've also been given the opportunity to partner with Ms. Regina Sunshine as a virtual camp counselor for her Awesome Girl Academy Summer Bridge Program. Things like this give me comfort that I'm on the right track. It gives me hope that I will one day discover and achieve my ultimate dream.

This is why I think everyone should dream. It gives you that push and in turn, you start to push yourself and reach heights that you would not have ever thought of. Maybe one day I will be that doctor I met when I was six or maybe I will direct movies with your favorite young black actors and actresses in the cast. I'm not really sure. However, I know that whatever it is, I want it to be something that leaves me feeling fulfilled.

Affirmations

I will be better today than the day before.
I will have a great day.
I will find reasons to smile today.
I will never settle.
I will succeed.

Bio

Makayla Coleman is originally from Alabama, and currently resides in Georgia. She is a junior in high school, and is a part of DECA Inc., National Honor Society, and the Future Business Leaders of America. She enjoys playing softball and throwing shot. Makayla also tutors kids ages 5 - 12 in math. During her down time, she enjoys watching television, listening to music, and coloring because they allow her to relax. Some of the dreams Makayla wishes to pursue after high school include sports medicine, interior design, or something in the entertainment industry.

CHAPTER 14

ZOE PATSY GORE

Age: 16

When Girls Dream

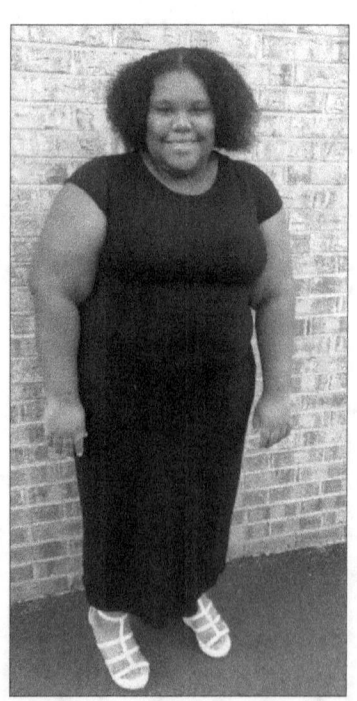

When I dream, I dream of changing the world, and here is how. I dream of changing the world by telling these queens and kings of the world to stop putting others down through actions such as bullying. I want to change the world by coming together and staying together. I want people to say about me, "I admire this woman and here are how her dreams made an impact on the world." I believe dreams are important for girls because our dreams matter. We can change the world, and we are in it together. Some girls' dreams are strong and powerful. We have to remind ourselves to be strong and continue to walk in the path of Jesus Christ.

I believe in the power of dreams simply because dreams can turn into something for the better, and the more you dream the better outcome will benefit you and the other strong amazing girls that are dreaming just like us. When you dream, make goals and standards from it. Your dreams can turn into life goals. They're like a bucket list. Your dreams can turn into your life's work and other things in life. Your dreams can bring you money depending on how you use them and make the best out of them.

I love my dreams because I hold them tight. I strongly believe my dreams will come true in so many different ways. Turn your dreams into some things you can go back and look at and say, "Wow, I did it! I made a dream of mine come true."

Affirmations
1. No matter how foggy the day might look or how you may not be able to see it, keep pushing and make sure to keep your head up.
2. Never look down and be ashamed of what you accomplished in your life on your dreams.
3. Love your dreams never look back on something good that made your dreams come true.

Bio
Zoe Patsy Gore is the daughter of Thomas Earl and Geraldine Gore and is the youngest of five girls. She is a tenth grader at South Columbus High School in Tabor City, NC and attends Mitchell Sea Missionary Baptist Church in Green Sea, SC. Zoe enjoys singing in the church choir, being a part of the praise and worship team and dancing on the church praise team. Zoe also enjoys working with the youth at Finklea Community Center. She plans to attend North Carolina A& T State University to pursue a career as a psychologist.

Official Awesome Girl Poem

When you see her know that she is Awesome.
So Awesome she blossoms like a flower.
She has power and stands tall like a tower.
She was built to empower.
When you see her know that she is Awesome.

Her beauty comes from within,
Just where it's always been.
She's motivated to reach new heights,
Removing all obstacles with love, power and might.
When you see her know that she is Awesome.

The girl with the big dreams,
Who chases after them by all means,
Determined, motivated, elevated all in one,
Everything she does will pay off in the long run.
When you see her know that she is Awesome.

A girl who knows her worth,
Chosen for this journey from birth,
She lets her inner light shine,
And gets better each mountain she climbs.
When you see her know that she is Awesome.

She's your next doctor, lawyer, author, scholar.
She's the next Maya Angelou or Madame CJ Walker.
She's full of fire,
Someone you can admire.
She'll inspire the world.
She's one phenomenal girl.
When you see her know that she is Awesome.

Written by: AnTonia Williams
www.AnToniaMFWilliams.com

Regina Sunshine's Awesome Girl Affirmations

I was born to win.

I am more than a conqueror.

I was created for greatness.

I was born to be victorious.

I will achieve my dreams.

I can be anything I choose.

I can do anything I set my mind to.

I am a champion.

I am worthy of the best things in life.

I am worthy of the dreams in my heart.

I am worthy of living a great life.

I AM AN AWESOME GIRL.

A Letter from Regina to You, Awesome Girl!

From My Heart to Yours,

Once again, our Awesome Girls have shared their hearts and their dreams with you. I hope you were inspired and that your dreams where ignited. Keep dreaming. Dream more. Dream bigger. And dream forever. It is our dreams that keep pushing us forward and light up our days. We hope you will share your dreams on the next pages. All it takes is one dream to change the world, and you just might be the dreamer the world is waiting for.

Be Blessed. Keep Winning!

Regina Sunshine

Author: _____

Age: _____

When Girls Dream:

Affirmations

1. _____

_____

2. _____

_____

3. _____

_____

4. _____

_____

5. _____

_____

6. _____

_____

7. _____

_____

8. _____

_____

9. _____

_____

10. _____

_____

When Girls Dream

BOOK SPONSOR

SHOE FETISH MOVEMENT

The Shoe Fetish Movement encourages and supports girls and women to know their self-worth, increase self-esteem through self-awareness, and gain confidence...an empowerment meeting/seminar with a flair. These qualities enable people to make better life choices, and stronger women mean stronger communities. Contact us for your next speaking event/meeting, 888-321-9604.

ABOUT THE CURATOR

Regina Sunshine Robinson is an Author, Motivational Speaker, Talk Show Host, Empowerment Coach, Corporate Trainer, and Teacher. She is the CEO of the Regina Sunshine Global Network, parent company to everything Regina Sunshine including EWATE, a Women's Empowerment Organization whose main purpose is to empower and encourage women to be all they were created to be in order to fulfill God's perfect plan for their lives. Regina is also the founder of the virtual Awesome Girl Academy and has dreams of having a brick and mortar school one day. Her personal motto is "It's Not Over Til I Win" and she wins when she sees others "WINNING". For more information, go to ReginaSunshine.com.

www.ingramcontent.com/pod-product-compliance
Lightning Source LLC
LaVergne TN
LVHW051511070426
835507LV00022B/3053